Teen Boy Problems
and How to Solve Them

Alex Hooper-Hodson

WAYLAND

Dedicated to Mum and Dad for their lifelong support.
Thanks to Greg, Manfie, Matt & Tall Oli for being the best friends I ever had.

First published in 2014 by Wayland
Copyright © Wayland 2014

Wayland
338 Euston Road
London NW1 3BH

Wayland Australia
Level 17/207
Kent Street
Sydney, NSW 2000

Commissioning editor: Debb
Design & illustration: Simon
Consultant: Anita Naik
Proofreader: Carron Brown

Dewey ref: 646.7'008351-dc23
ISBN 978 0 7502 8104 41
eBook ISBN 978 0 7502 8580 3

Printed in China

10 9 8 7 6 5 4 3 2 1

Wayland is a division of Hachette Children's Books,
an Hachette UK company.

www.hachette.co.uk

Falkirk Council	
Askews & Holts	2014
J646.7	£6.99

The website addresses (URLs) included in this book were valid at the time of going to press. However, it is possible that contents or addresses may have changed since the publication of this book. No responsibility for any such changes can be accepted by either the author or the Publisher.

Contents

A Word From Alex Hooper-Hodson

As a teenager you have the best seat in the house for one of the most exciting stages of life. So why would you need to read a book about it? Why shouldn't you just live your life and figure out your problems as you go along? Well, you can, of course. But the problem is that being a teenager can involve making some very important decisions – and things can get pretty hairy if you make the wrong ones.

With this in mind I have selected the 52 most common teen boy problems I've come across in my career as an agony uncle. I've provided solutions to each of them and next steps to take to ensure you come out the other side. In the cases where the problem is too big to solve on your own, I've advised where you can seek further help. There is a Get Connected! section on pages 94–95 with a list of agencies who can help you with almost any issue that you might come across in your teens.

However, please don't assume that all of these 52 problems are likely to happen to you – they're not. But by pre-arming yourself with knowledge, you'll know exactly what to do if and when a problem does raise its head. Some of the areas I cover, like how to be confident and raise your self-esteem or how to negotiate the perils of online social media, are huge life issues so it's good to have some guidance on these things. So read on, and good luck with your teens. I hope this book helps make them the best years of your life!

Alex Hooper-Hodson

Boys & Their Bodies

Alex says

Boys have body issues...

As a teenage boy, your body is growing and changing at a pace, often making you self-conscious and ultra-aware of every spot, or other parts of your body that you are unhappy with or that might seem to behave in odd ways. You might be experiencing uncalled-for erections at the most difficult moments or finding yourself thinking about sex most of the day (and night). You might be asking yourself such questions as: Am I too short? Is my penis the right size? Do I smell? or just, Am I NORMAL?

Teens are also bombarded by images in the media that are impossible to live up to. Think about all those super-muscled torsos you see advertising anything from aftershave to hair products, as well as featured in online games, music videos and in social media. These messages can sometimes convey the idea that we are too fat, too thin, not muscly enough, not strong, tall or 'manly' enough. As a result, boys can stress about how people view them, and go to great lengths to project an ideal image to outsiders. Much time gets devoted to the clothes you're wearing and also your body shape. In some cases, body consciousness gets taken to extremes, and some boys start going to the gym in an effort to bulk up their muscles, and start buying supplements intended for adults – that aren't necessarily healthy even for adults!

The sudden interest in your appearance usually occurs around the age of about 13, though it can start before. However, there's no coincidence that this thought process coincides with puberty. That's right, you start to care more about what you look like and comparing yourself to others – just when you start to leave childhood. Ironically, it's the same moment that your body decides to sabotage your appearance with pimples, unwanted hair and body odours, and your sexual feelings can cause you embarrassment at the trickiest times!

There are also concerns about starting to shave and what is the best method to use. These issues vary with ethnic background as some boys are darker haired than others, or have hair that is coarser or naturally more curly. Should you start using deodorant straight away? It's probably important to visit the dentist at this stage too, to ensure your teeth are healthy or see if you need any corrective procedures (like fitting braces or retainers). Straightening teeth while you are still growing is easier than when you reach adulthood.

This chapter not only explores the range of bodily issues that we boys agonise about in our most private moments; but it also proposes some realistic solutions. While it's completely normal to feel vulnerable and have anxieties about your looks and appearance, there are loads of healthy ways to make you feel better about them, too. For nearly every problem there is a solution.

1 I'm tired of my parents treating me like a kid!

I'm so fed up with my mum — she treats me like a little kid. She still talks to me like she did when I was seven, but my voice has broken, I need to shave every couple of weeks and I have a girlfriend! How long is it going to take for mum to wake up to the fact that I'm not a child anymore? It's not just about the way she talks to me either — she won't let me put a lock on my bedroom door, she still thinks it's OK to walk in on me in the bathroom and she wants me in bed by 10pm. I'm getting fed up with it now and feel I really need some privacy — can you help?

Mack, 14

Alex says

I hear your frustration. I think many of us have felt the same. From your perspective, childhood is done. There's no going back. But while you aren't the little boy your mum sees, you're not an adult yet. Growing up is still going to take some time and some more life experience. As for your mum, it's hard for parents to keep up to speed with their children's development and to know how to behave towards them. In other words, the hormones that change your life at this time act a good deal faster than your mum's ability to adjust her outlook. The chief of these hormones – testosterone – is also responsible for making you feel more wilful and independent. Your body is telling you that you are a man despite the fact it's not entirely true yet. If you want your mum to start seeing you as more adult, then be patient with her. Yes, you need to remind her that you are no longer seven years old, you can't be expected to share all your secrets and that you think she should knock on the bedroom or bathroom door before entering as a matter of courtesy. But you also need to demonstrate through your actions that you are getting there, and try to greet confrontation in a calm and rational way. The penny will drop soon enough that you are no longer her baby boy!

I think the fact that your parents don't let you lock your door shows that they really don't understand what you're going through. Puberty is difficult enough already without even having a bit of privacy in your own bedroom. Speak to your mum again.
Frankie, 15

Just look at it this way: you shave and you have a girlfriend! Your mum will come round to seeing things your way in the end but in the meantime be proud of yourself because it sounds like you're dealing with puberty pretty well.
Chris, 16

Be patient with your mum. I know it seems unfair, but in the end she'll adjust to you growing up. It can be hard for parents because they spend so much time looking after you that they sometimes forget you need to be independent too.
Jas, 14

2 I don't recognise myself in the mirror any more!

Something's happened to me and I can't describe how exactly. It's like whenever I look in the mirror I don't recognise the person I see. My face looks a bit different and I'm starting to see lines that weren't there before, changes to my skin and spots where I didn't used to have them. I was never the kind who spent time examining himself in the mirror and I don't think I was ever this conscious of what I looked like, but now it's all I think about!

Elyas, 13

Alex says

Yes, your body is changing! The changes are subtle at first: your skin becomes temporarily more oily and prone to acne. Your features will gradually mature and change shape as you develop. You will get taller, your voice will break and you'll grow more body hair. Puberty not only causes physical changes but also makes you super-aware of them. Puberty often brings with it an awareness of your image for the first time. These developments can seem worrying at first but it's perfectly normal to feel this way – and remember everyone else is feeling them, too! Just relax and let things happen in their own way. Try not to focus too much on yourself and your body changes. Puberty will happen in its own sweet way, so make sure you keep up with your hobbies and interests, and that you don't miss out on living your life and having fun in the meantime!

3 They're teasing me for being overweight. Please help!

The boys at school are making my life a misery because of my weight. It was a bit of a shock when they started calling me names as I never thought of myself as fat, or really even cared what I looked like. I would do anything to go back to being my old self when I was a bit thinner. Why has this happened to me and is there anything I can do to get back to the weight I was before I hit 14?

Kumar, 14

Alex says

One reason why you may have gained weight is that puberty hormones can alter your metabolism. Where once you were fairly slim, your body may now store more fat to help you grow. But if you become less active at the same time, this makes you gain weight. Luckily, this isn't usually an extreme difference and can be combated by eating healthily and staying as active as you can (this includes exercise and sport). Check the labels on the foods you eat and try to eat sensibly. For example, just switching from a burger and chips to a baked potato with baked beans or salad would save you a load of calories. If you're really concerned, your GP can advise you on weight loss and provide you with diet plans, too. In the meantime, if the boys carry on bullying you in this way, talk to your mum and teacher about what's happening. Verbal bullying is a serious issue and can damage your self-confidence, which is why it needs to be dealt with swiftly by your school. Also please check out the Get Connected! section on pages 94-95 for organisations that can help you with this.

Exercise – why it's worth the sweat!

Whether you love exercise and sport or not, it really pays to bring it into your life in your teens. Even if you're more interested in the game itself (for instance, football or tennis) than the benefits to your body, it's worth knowing why it's worth breaking out into a sweat.

The physical benefits of exercise are the more obvious ones. Puberty brings with it the potential to put on more weight and regular exercise will help you burn the calories that may otherwise contribute to weight gain. If you exercise regularly, you are more likely to stay at a healthy weight and have more energy on a daily basis. Exercise and staying active also helps you start to strengthen your new muscles as they develop.

Regular aerobic exercise, such as running, tennis, football or rugby, makes your muscles use oxygen more efficiently and strengthens your heart and lungs. However, powerlifting, competitive weightlifting, and bodybuilding are not recommended for teens who are still maturing. That's because these types of activity can cause serious injuries to growing bones, muscles and joints. Note, though, that you can strength train at any age.

The more often you exercise the fitter you will be, which is great for your overall health and body, but not all of the benefits of exercise are just physical ones. Exercise is also mood-enhancing and makes you feel good; it makes you walk taller and be more self-confident; and it improves your posture and general wellbeing. Overall you are more likely to have a positive self-image.

Numerous research studies have shown that exercise can make you happier, more grounded and more capable of dealing with the everyday worries, stress or anxiety of school, homework and exams. If you exercise you are more likely to have a good night's sleep and wake up feeling rested and able to apply yourself the next day.

The reason for this is that during exercise, our bodies release chemicals called endorphins each time we get our heart rate up for a prolonged time. So, just to give you a practical example, 30 minutes of running or walking at a good pace, 3 times a week, can get you back on track if you've been stressing about school or worrying about looming exams.

The next time you feel overwhelmed by schoolwork or disagreements with parents, or generally feel that life and all that stuff is getting on top of you — then give exercise a go. Getting sweaty may seem like the last thing you want to do but, trust me, if you give it a chance and let it do its thing, exercise will dramatically change your mood and give a long-term boost to your body!

4 Do I need to start shaving?

I'm fair-skinned and dark-haired. Am I supposed to know when I should start shaving? I've noticed hair is appearing on my cheeks and there's some dark hair on my top lip. It's not that long but the other day my dad made a joke about it. I wondered if I should start shaving it, and if so, how? And once I start shaving is it something I have to do every day? It's not easy to ask my family for advice because they all make jokes about personal stuff.

Tao, 14

Alex says

Jokes aside, perhaps you should try asking your dad — because he will almost certainly have lots of information he could pass on. In regard to whether you should start shaving, have you got enough hair on your face yet to merit a full shave? Simple test — if it's fine and downy, I shouldn't bother. If it feels more like the tougher hairs on your head, then get cracking. You'll obviously need a razor and some shaving foam. There are lots of expensive kits on the market but as long as what you get is sharp (please be very careful!) you'll manage. Wet your skin; spread shaving foam across the areas where the hair is growing and shave with downward strokes. Shaving upwards can remove stubborn hairs but is more likely to leave you with a rash or cuts. Go gently and don't press too hard. Let the blade travel over the skin under its own weight rather than use it like a veg peeler! When you're finished douse your face with cold water as this helps close the pores, as does a splash of a post-shave balm.

5 They call me 'pizza face'! How can I get clear skin?

Luke, 13

I've got terrible acne. All my school friends have started calling me 'pizza face', which hurts my feelings and none of the girls will talk to me. It's really upsetting as my skin was never a problem when I was younger. I've tried squeezing the spots but it just makes them redder and leaves scars. I feel really bad about myself and my confidence is really low. I don't want to leave the house anymore and have given up on the idea of ever having a girlfriend. Is there anything I can do to make my spots less noticeable or to clear them up entirely? I'll do anything!

Alex says

All teenagers suffer from spots to varying degrees, but there are things you can do to help combat acne and get your confidence and your self-esteem back on track. Spots at this age result directly from the hormonal changes going on it your body. Pores and hair follicles get blocked due to excess sebum (your body's natural oils), then bacteria infect the area and spots occur. Acne and spots can destroy your confidence especially when silly name-calling happens (make sure you tell them how much it upsets you) but you can help yourself by trying over-the-counter acne treatments (ask your local pharmacist for advice). If after a month these don't work then it's best to make an appointment to see your GP. Acne is a medical condition and can be treated with a prescription from your doctor, such as a course of antibiotics. These can take about 6 months to work so hang in there.

It Happened to Me

I first started to suffer from acne when I was 12. It covered my cheeks, forehead and nose and looked like a terrible angry rash. The only problem was it never went away. Everyone talked about me at school and it definitely affected my friendships as some people didn't want to be seen with me. I would squeeze the worst spots but as there were so many I was told not to do this as it could leave bad scars. It was painful, too — red and sore and no amount of spot lotions or remedies seemed to bring any relief, even the ones suggested to me by the pharmacist. I went to my GP and he prescribed me with a course of antibiotics. It consisted of tablets and an antibiotic cream to rub into my skin. At first it didn't seem to work and I started to lose hope, but after a few months of regular usage I noticed a slight change. Within another month my acne had begun to disappear and I started to feel a whole lot better about myself. That whole chapter of my life is like a bad dream now but I wanted to share the story because I know there are other people out there in the same position.

Jay, 14

6 I'm much shorter than all my friends!

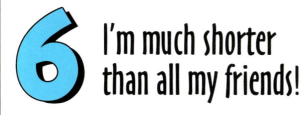

David, 12

I'm 13 and the shortest in my class. I'm 1.6m and always getting picked on. Two years ago I was the same height as all the other boys but since then they've all grown taller. It's making me unhappy and I worry that I'm never going to get a girlfriend because I'm so short. I used to like playing sport but I'm hardly ever picked for teams now and I think it's because of my height. Is there anything I can do to grow more?

Alex says

When we're going through puberty, there are many things that can undermine our self-esteem. While it's easy to assume that only tall boys get girlfriends and are successful in sport, logic says this isn't true (footballers come in a variety of heights, as do runners). Also, there's no evidence that girls pick boyfriends based on height. Of course, it isn't always easy to feel confident if everyone is towering above you. But rest assured you are unlikely to stay at 1.6m for long. All teens experience a growth spurt. It may start around age 11 but could happen as late as your early teens. In some cases, growth continues well into your 20s – as does brain development. So, while you feel the other boys around you are powering ahead, the height you are now is almost certainly not the height you'll stay. In the meantime, carry on playing sport because it will increase your confidence. Stay active and eat well – your body will do the rest. If you are still worried in 6 months' time, visit your GP who should be able to reassure you.

7 I'm worried my penis may be too small

Kier, 14

> Sometimes after PE we take showers together and all the boys make jokes about each other's bodies. Some boys get picked on for being overweight, skinny or having spotty backs. I've noticed over the last year that all the other boys have much bigger penises than I do. I know it's only a matter of time before someone spots it and they all start joking about me. Please help!

Alex says

Many boys and even grown men worry about penis size. So it's worth bearing in mind the average penis length when erect is between 12–17cm (5 inches and 7 inches). If you're anywhere in this range and still a teenager, then you're already average for a grown man. But even if you aren't bigger than 17cm (5 inches) now, please don't worry. Neither of the functions of a penis require it to be a certain length (peeing and making babies). Boys, as you've realised, love to make jokes about each other's 'body issues' so my advice is just to ignore it. Also bear in mind that coldness, exercise and anxiety tends to reduce the blood flow to the penis, thus making it smaller, so a post-PE shower experience isn't the best time to judge anything.

✺ **DO** Stop worrying about your size.

✺ **DON'T** Let comments from others affect you.

8 My feet smell really bad. What can I do to stop it?

Kurt, 14

I am worried about my feet. They always smell awful and I don't know how to make them stop. I have a shower every morning but by lunchtime I can smell my feet. I get really paranoid around girls and if someone comments on the 'bad eggs' smell that is lurking around I usually blame it on something else. I'm running out of excuses now so please give me some advice that will actually work as I'm desperate.

Alex says

Your feet start to smell when you sweat into your shoes and then don't let them dry properly before putting them on again. As a teenager you have greater sweat production due to the changes your body is going through. So while the good news is that this condition isn't likely to be a life-long thing, you need to be prepared for it to be around for a while. If you want to beat it, you need to get into a routine of scrubbing your feet each morning and night in soap and water, not just letting them get wet. Spray your feet with antiperspirant or try insoles that are designed to deodorise your shoes or even ventilated sports socks. Also ask your parents if they would invest in a second pair of school shoes for you. By having two pairs of shoes you can take turns letting one pair dry while you wear the other. Never wear either pair for more than two days in a row. If you do this, not only will you prolong the lifespan of the shoes but you will also notice they no longer smell so bad. If you are still experiencing problems in a couple of weeks or so, contact your GP.

9 I get teased at school for wearing glasses

> Last week my teacher asked me to read something on the white board and after watching me squint for a few minutes he told me to get my eyes tested. It turns out that I'm short-sighted. My mum refuses to pay for contact lenses (or laser eye-surgery!) and so now I have to wear glasses every day to school. I really don't like them because they make me feel ugly and everyone says I look better without them. What can I do?

Olly, 13

Alex says

It takes time to get used to wearing glasses. At first, they feel strange on your face and you can be self-conscious, but these days glasses are also really fashionable and can really become part of your 'look'. Think about celebrities like Johnny Depp, Ryan Gosling and Justin Timberlake – they all wear specs. And as I am sure you'll agree, squinting is never a cool look, and being able to see the board in school is also good for your education and your future. So be bold, be confident and make glasses part of your style. Take a friend along to the opticians who can advise you on the best frames to suit your shape of face. If your mum doesn't want to pay for contact lenses because they are pricey then so be it, but perhaps you could start to save up for contact lenses and suggest them to your mum in another year or so? Laser eye-surgery is also expensive but surgeons won't do it until you're 21 anyway, so you have a few years to wait if you decide to go down that route.

10

Is it OK to use protein shakes to help me bulk up?

> I used to get picked on at school for being 'weedy'. When I turned 16, I decided to do something about it and began going to the gym to work out. One of the personal trainers there told me that protein supplements would help me bulk up my muscles. He says there is no point in working out without them. But he's not a doctor or even a nutritionist so is he qualified to be giving this advice?

Jamie, 16

Alex says

Your personal trainer is wrong; lifting weights has an impact whether you take protein supplements or not. He is simply echoing a view popular among some adults who train a lot, that protein supplements are essential. There is nothing wrong with these shakes and drinks except that they are made for adults and are very expensive. At 16 there are still an awful lot of changes going on in your body and you're right not to mess about and start taking supplements that you don't feel comfortable with. Tell him you're not interested in hearing any more about protein shakes and if you do want to up the protein content in your diet focus on eating things like tuna, eggs and chicken – all of which are great sources of protein.

Puberty – what's happening to me?

Puberty can be a tricky time for teens in terms of their body image. As some of my letters have shown, things don't always go smoothly during this stage in your life, but I'd like to offer you some reassurance. No matter whether you have smelly feet, acne or are worried about your size in any way – rest assured that every other teen who is going through puberty has also got their own issues going on.

What's important to realise is that puberty is a process that your body and mind go through over a number of years. With each new physical change and hormonal push (the reason why your body and feelings change so much) you are going to feel different. Sometimes angry, sometimes moody, sometimes you'll feel frustrated or you will feel all of this and more. The key is to give yourself a break!

Puberty is tough and you need to take things day by day and reassure yourself that the way you look and feel now isn't the way you'll look and feel five years from now. What's more, talk to someone about how you're feeling, especially if you're worried, because you don't have to deal with it on your own.

Thinking about it, when you put puberty into perspective you are actually a hero. Wait – don't fall about laughing! What I mean is that when adults face problems in life they generally have a lot more experience to fall back on. But you have to cope with puberty at a very difficult age, with a whole lot of other pressures going on in life too, including school life, friends and your relationship with your family.

This is also the time of your life when you are probably going to feel most alienated from your body, and the most uncoordinated. And there are good reasons for this. Your body is growing in spurts (literally growth spurts) which can mean that for short periods of time your limbs and torso don't really work in sync anymore, your coordination may be off and you may bump into things or trip over more.

You may have to learn how to move again, how to balance – you even have to learn how to use your vocal chords again. You are going through one of the biggest changes of your life and it's something that people don't always give you enough credit for. So give yourself a medal!

It's no surprise then that this phase of life produces lots of false starts and potential crises. We all learn by having experiences. These help us decide which things we want to do again and which are better avoided in the future. It's only therefore by trying new things, and making mistakes, that we discover who we really are. Our personalities are forged amid all the worry and confusion.

The next time you feel inadequate because puberty seems to have left you behind, or frustrated because it won't leave you alone, I want you to take a step back and reassure yourself that things are going to be fine. You are coping with enormous changes in your life and you are doing fantastically well. Many adults have forgotten their own struggles at the same age – which is why they may not always appear to understand. Talking to the adults in your life will remind them of this stage. Good luck, go forth and enjoy being a teen!

11 I'm obsessed with losing weight. Do I have an eating disorder?

Dan, 15

A few months ago some boys started commenting on the size of my stomach, so I started running every day and I mostly cut out breakfast, lunch and all junk food. I lost a lot of weight. Now my mum and my friends have started to say I looked too thin. The problem is I don't think I'm thin at all. I still think my stomach is big and I still think I need to lose weight. I'm worried I may have an eating disorder – or if I do actually have a weight issue.

Alex says

It's hard to say from your letter if you have an eating disorder, like anorexia, which is why you should see GP as soon as possible. He or she will be able to weigh you and tell you whether you need to lose weight or gain weight, so I urge you to make the appointment today. One meal a day is not enough for any one, let alone a teenager who is still growing and developing. Aside from not giving you enough energy this lack of food is starving your body of nutrients just when you need most need it. If it transpires that you do need to lose weight, your GP will be able to provide you with diet sheets to help you do it in a healthy way. Please bear in mind that while exercise is excellent for you, being obsessive about running every day isn't. If you do find yourself obsessively dieting, despite what your GP says, please go back and see him or her again and get some further advice. Look up Beat in the Get Connected! section on page 95. They run online support and help for anyone with this kind of problem.

The F*
Word

*(Feelings)

Alex says

Emotions and how to handle them!

Since entering your teens, have you noticed yourself losing your temper and wondering why? Or have you had days where you've woken up feeling sad and moody for no apparent reason? It might be because of the changes your body is going through or it could be down to the stress of dealing with your new stage in life. Whatever the root causes, it can be a real help to use some practical strategies when these unexpected and strong emotions take over.

The most important thing is to be self aware. As very young children we possessed little insight into our feelings, but acted them out in our behaviour. Now that you're a bit older, this is not so. You can recognise an emotion when you're feeling it. So as soon as you do this, put a name to it! By naming an emotion you're one step nearer to controlling it. For instance, if you realise you are in an angry mood then you know a temporary solution is to bite your tongue and give yourself the time to calm down. The same goes for feeling sad – take a step back and tell yourself this problem won't last forever. This process helps you keep a sense of control over your emotions. Of course, some emotions can be very upsetting to acknowledge but it's necessary if you want to recover.

People who block their feelings may make their problems worse. It uses up energy. And bad feelings are hard to change if they never get ventilated. But what you may find is that as soon as you discuss your problem with a family member or sympathetic friend, it takes on a different colour. Your perspective alters. Often the only way to get to the root cause of our troubles is to put them into words. Not only does this give us a sense of proportion, the very process of talking about it actually relaxes us.

There are, of course, other ways you can work through these trapped feelings. Music or creativity are brilliant ways to express yourself. Or simply going for a brisk walk, going for a run or kicking a football around with some mates for half an hour while thinking things through, can really help you to put things in perspective. Finally try not to be too self-critical. Almost everyone from time to time has trouble with their emotions. Be patient and kind to yourself and your negative feelings will pass. If they persist, start to get worse, start to interfere with your life, get you in trouble or you start to feel out of control a lot of the time, then it's time to speak to your GP. He or she will be able to help you get on top of things so that you feel more in control of your emotions, rather than letting them control you.

12 How can I learn to become confident with people?

My best friend is super-confident. He has no problem approaching girls and chatting to them like they are old friends. At parties he can approach a group of strangers and soon he'll be on first name terms with all of them. I'm usually sat in the corner on my own. It's not that I want to be anti-social but I find I'm only really confident when it's one on one. As soon as I'm faced with a group (it can be boys or girls) I just want to run away! Is there anything you can recommend that can help me boost my confidence?

Max, 14

Alex says

The difference between you and your best friend is that he has self-belief, and at the moment, you don't. But don't despair because you can develop it! Becoming self-confident is a process that you can start by filling your mind with positive and self-affirming thoughts. Tell yourself that you're attractive, interesting and successful – imagine these things the moment you enter the room. It doesn't matter if deep down you don't really feel this way, because if you act confident, other people will see you as confident. This in turn will boost your self-esteem. And then one day you'll realise that you no longer have to pretend and you truly feel good about yourself!

As a first step, be brave and seek out a social situation that you would normally avoid. When meeting someone new, look them straight in the eye and introduce yourself with a bright smile and in a confident tone. Next, hold a conversation all the while giving yourself positive reassurance in your mind. Even if you have only that one conversation, it will boost your self-confidence. The next time you're out try it again. Take baby steps and with some practice your confidence will blossom. Good luck!

Confidence is a state of mind. I used to be really shy and found it really hard to talk to people. But I forced myself to believe in ME and now it's second nature!
Tavi 15

You don't have to be the life and the soul of the party. It is OK to be a little shy sometimes. Just don't let it get you down and don't compare yourself to other people.
Dan, 14

Talking to girls is much easier than it seems. Just be real and be yourself. If they think you're boring, then you're probably talking to the wrong girl!
Kai, 14

You've got to believe you're every bit as good as your friend – because you are!
Simeon, 15

13 Schoolwork is totally stressing me out!

At the moment I'm getting really stressed all the time with schoolwork. My friends seem to be able to stop it getting on top of them, but I have this feeling that my work is getting out of control. I stress out at school and then I stress about homework when I get home. If I've got a test the next day I just can't stop thinking about it. Please help me because I'm not even at GCSE stage yet!

Nicolai, 13

Alex says

Stress can be an issue in your teens and so it's good to develop strategies for dealing with it as soon as possible. One of the best ways to deal with stress is to feel in control, and to aim to structure your day. Make a list and break down the tasks you have to achieve into a series of manageable chunks. The more organised you are, the less you will worry about what it is you're meant to be doing next. This in turn will help you focus on the task that's in front of you and you won't feel the need to rush. Make sure you take regular breaks from schoolwork so you can return feeling refreshed, and reward yourself when you've worked hard. Meet up with a friend or do something else you enjoy. Exercise and regular meals can help reduce stress levels, too, as can making sure you get a good sleep each night. So make sure these feature high on your list.

14

I spend a lot of time on my own. Does it mean I'm depressed?

> My mum said to me last night that she's worried I might be depressed. She wants me to see our GP to talk about how I'm feeling. I think she's overreacting and I really don't like the idea of having someone asking me lots of questions. She says I'm moody and withdrawn and that I spend too much time in my bedroom on my own playing online games. Do you think I am depressed?

Chi, 14

Alex says

Your mum is right to be concerned about you as depression can strike in the teen years and needs to be addressed in order that it doesn't become a bigger issue. If you have been feeling low for more than a few days or have lost interest in things that you used to enjoy, then you might need help. What you see as just 'playing games online' may be a symptom of being unhappy. But it's also true that puberty muddles your emotions and can make you feel down, and it's not unusual for teenage boys to spend time alone gaming. I would say that if there's a doubt in your mind, then it can't hurt for you to go and talk to your GP. Your mum may be acting cautiously here but depression can be a serious issue, so it's best not to take the chance.

Bullies, cyberbullies and other bigmouths

Many of us have experienced bullying either directly or indirectly. Despite public awareness of bullying, it continues in schools and online on a daily basis and can be a tough issue for parents and teachers to tackle. Teens who get bullied rarely wish to talk about it for fear of suffering reprisals, but also because bullying breaks your confidence and makes you feel shamed into silence. This is why it's essential to speak up and be heard if it's happening to you. Speaking out is the only way to stop the bullying, stop feeling scared and find help to rebuild your confidence.

Bullying can take many forms including physical assault, teasing, name calling, cyberbullying and making threats. It can be aimed at people because of their race, religion, gender or sexual orientation, or for no reason at all.

Cyberbullying is what happens when a bully uses social media, a mobile phone or any other device to carry out their attacks. If you thought that because cyberbullying takes place in a virtual environment it is any less serious – then think again. Cyberbullying has the ability to leave the school playground and follow the victim into their home, rendering them vulnerable to the bullies not just during a school day, but 24/7!

Just so you're clear bullying includes all of the following: calling someone rude names, hurting someone physically, taking an object or money from someone by force, damaging someone's property, hacking someone's social media account and impersonating them with a view to causing them trouble, sending rude or offensive texts or emails, making repeated and nasty prank calls, threats and intimidation, frightening someone into doing what you tell them or scaring someone so much they don't want to go to school. Even making silent phone calls and then hanging up can be classed as bullying if it's felt to be threatening.

Many of the perpetrators of bullying do so because they are unhappy in their own lives and want to feel powerful, just for a moment, by making you feel helpless. The best way to defeat a bully is to immediately talk to a teacher or a parent. Bullies stop when they're exposed.

If you're being bullied or cyberbullied, there are a number of things to remember:

1 You have to speak up as it won't stop if you keep quiet.

2 Keep a record of everything that happens as evidence (for example you should screenshot bullying text messages/instant messages/social media messages and save them).

3 If it's happening at school get your parents to ensure that an anti-bullying procedure is being followed and that you meet regularly to discuss what's happening.

4 If you are being threatened or physically attacked outside of school then you need to involve the police.

5 If it's happening online or via apps take a two-week (or longer) tech break so no one can reach you.

6 If you are suffering anonymous online bullies there are still a range of ways to stop the abuse (see the Get Connected! section on pages 94–95 for more information).

It Happened to Me

Between the ages of six and 14, I was badly teased at school. I was already 44kg by the age of eight. I hated it, but hated the taunts even more. Loads of kids in my year would join in and there was nothing I could do to stop them. By the time my 14th birthday came around, I decided to change everything and with help from my mum and the doctor I went on a diet. The fat started to drop away as I began walking to and from school every day. For the first time in my life I felt like I no longer had to be the victim. But although I wasn't overweight anymore, the years of bullying had made a lasting impression on me. I guess I still felt like a fat boy pretending to be thin. If the word 'fat' comes up in a conversation, I always think people are referring to me. I suppose that's why I later chose to pick on other boys who were overweight. I felt like I was the one with the power now and the roles were finally reversed. It didn't occur to me that what I was doing was bullying. If anyone knew what it was like to be bullied it was me, yet here I was giving someone else a really hard time. That made me feel ashamed of myself.

Lee, 16

15

My parents expect me to choose between them!

Milo, 13

I found out a few months ago that my parents are getting a divorce. The arguments in our house have been terrible for years, and for a long time I was really down about them splitting up. It got so bad that I stopped going to school, so then I got in trouble. When my parents found out, we all sat down and they told me they would always love and care for me no matter what happened between them. They also said that I'd still get to see them both. The only thing that's still bothering is that they are telling me it's my choice which one of them I choose to live with. It's breaking my heart to think that I might have to choose between them. Have you had a letter like this before, and if so, can you help?

Alex says

Divorce is a painful process for everyone, but I'm glad your parents made it clear that none of this was your fault and that they broke up for their own reasons. I know it feels like you are being asked to make impossible decisions because you need them both and you cannot split yourself in two, but there's no reason you can't experiment. Have you considered asking if you can go through a trial period of living with them in turn for a bit? It's clear you love them both a lot and so you don't have to view this in terms of choosing which one you love most. You might find that the dynamic of living with one of them suits you better than the other. The only way you'll really know this is by spending a bit of time living with each of them solo. Suggest this to them and explain the reasons behind it. They sound like caring and understanding parents who are likely to listen. Good luck.

16 My mates want me to do dangerous things for a laugh!

There isn't much to do in our village so a group of us meet down on the marshes near the train tracks. One of the games they play is sticking coins on the rails and seeing how flat the trains can make them. Another game they play is seeing how late they can leave it when the train's coming before running over the tracks. None of the trains go really fast so they say that it isn't all that dangerous, but I haven't done it yet and they are all putting pressure on me to do it next weekend.

The problem is, I've been waking up in a sweat at the thought of running across the lines, and it's all I can think about. They'll probably laugh at me if I don't do it. Please help, it's making me feel sick!

Damian, 14

Alex says

Firstly, I should tell you that trespassing on train tracks is illegal and you will get into trouble with the police. In this country last year, 50 people were killed while trespassing on the railways. So stop and think about this. Running in front of a 200-tonne machine hurtling towards you at any speed is a very bad idea indeed. The risk HUGE and in spite of what your friends say, it is VERY dangerous. Just imagine how easy it would be to slip on an oily sleeper or twist your ankle and not be able to move? A train can't stop in time.

Of course, I understand that peer pressure can be a powerful influence. We all want the respect of our friends – but they are dicing with death here. So do not risk your life to avoid being sneered at. Just tell them you are not up for the challenge because you value your life too much. Your friends are not only endangering their own lives, but possibly the lives of train passengers if one of their stupid pranks goes wrong. Think, also, that your parents would be heart-broken – as would your entire village if there was a tragedy caused by somebody's foolishness. I urge you to find somewhere else to hang around other than the railway tracks, and if they refuse to see your point of view then it may be time to find another crowd to be with.

Don't be a fool! Find something else to do or find a new group to hang out with. This is WRONG.
Kieran, 14

I knew a gang of kids who would jump from rooftops. One of them died doing it. If I was you, I'd get my parents involved.
Philip, 13

A group of lads in our town think it's amusing to run across the motorway. They are just playing with their lives!
Billy, 14

I know it can be hard when people are egging you on but you need to be the voice of reason for your group. Stand up to them and don't do it!
Nick, 15

17

I like fighting with other boys! Is this 'normal'?

I've started getting into lots of fights at school. At first it was over a couple of stupid arguments, but now I start them on purpose because I like the feeling it gives me. I enjoy the feeling of excitement I have when I get in a fight. I can't describe it but it's like being on a rollercoaster. I've been getting into loads of trouble at school but I don't know what will make me stop!

Joel, 13

Alex says

Fighting feels exhilarating because the body releases huge dose of a chemical called adrenaline into your bloodstream. This has the effect of 'turbo charging' you to help you win. The downside is that some people enjoy this sensation too much or it can become addictive. Getting into fights is not a habit you can continue indefinitely. The problem is one day you will either get hurt, or hurt someone badly and end up in serious trouble. And remember people don't want to make friends with a thug who fights all the time. Try to channel these urges into a sport like martial arts or boxing. This way you will still get to fight but these sports will teach you respect and control, and will most importantly give you the discipline and sense to not fight on the street.

✳ **DO** Learn to control your impulses.

✳ **DON'T** Act like a thug. It intimidates people and is unacceptable.

18 I'm obsessed with thoughts of death!

> I just found out that my favourite teacher is ill with cancer and ever since I heard the news I can't stop crying. I've never known anyone who has died. It's a horrible feeling to hear that someone might die – even if they are not that close to me. I wake up in the night thinking of all the ways I could die and I think I'm becoming quite obsessed with it. I wish I knew some way to put the happiness back into my life but everything just seems depressing at the moment.

Kane, 13

Alex says

You've had a big shock. This has put your brain into a spin and you are now thinking the worst about everything. It's extremely sad when someone gets seriously ill and I don't wish to belittle that. But please notice that all the rest of your world remains the same. Everyone else you know is OK – and so are you. Once you get your head around being sad, you will also find this event fits into your mind as 'another event' although it's unwanted. You also have to tell yourself not to jump the gun. Being diagnosed with cancer these days is far removed from getting a death sentence. A lot of cancers have a positive cure rate – in some cases as high as 80–90%. If you want to start putting the happiness back into your life, share your worries with someone you can trust. We all have these feelings sometimes and by sharing yours with someone, hopefully you will see start to see that you are not on your own with your feelings.

19

I don't feel safe at home since the burglary

My dad's new house was burgled last month. They took my step-mum's jewellery, the TV and computer and they completely wrecked his living room. He says it's secure now because he's put new locks on the doors and windows, but this doesn't reassure me as the locks didn't stop them the first time. I haven't been round there since the burglary and I certainly don't want to stay over. I don't understand how he can relax knowing it could happen again. Is there anything I can do to help me feel safe again?

Daryl, 14

Alex says

Burglary can be devastating. Losing your possessions is bad but having your space and safety invaded by strangers is often worse. Your dad did the right thing when he showed you he'd secured the house, but it's understandable if it takes you some time to feel comfortable being there again. Share your worries with your dad so that he understands the situation. Then look at the facts: presumably this is the first time you've experienced a burglary in your 14 years — so it's not a common event. Your dad could ask a crime prevention officer to come round and give you some advice on the best way to prevent further burglaries — this might help you to start to feel more secure in your dad's home. If your feelings continue beyond a few weeks, then visit the victim support website featured in the Get Connected! section on page 94. They can provide advice and support for people in your position and can help you get through this.

20 I can't stop thinking about sex. What should I do?

Please help me. All I seem to think about at the moment is sex. It's on my mind all the time, and even when I am at school I find myself thinking about it during class. I'm too embarrassed to say anything to my friends or my mum in case they think I'm weird.

Ash, 12

Alex says

Puberty is about more than physical changes. As your body grows into adulthood, your emotions and sexual feelings all increase and mature. As a result, you will find yourself becoming excited by images and ideas and feelings, and in many cases find yourself thinking about sex all the time. This is pretty normal and not something to worry about unless it's stopping you from doing the things you need to do (schoolwork) or want to do (hobbies and interests). The best way to switch off sexual thoughts is to focus on something else. Often, thinking about something quite serious – a person, a lesson, a TV programme – will help refocus your brain in the moment. Also consider talking to someone you trust about what's happening. I guarantee 90% of your friends feel the same way and just knowing this and hearing this from someone else can help put your mind at rest.

21

My brother is a troublemaker but I want to be like him!

Stefan, 12

> My older brother, who's 16, is always getting into trouble of one sort or another, but he's also really clever and likeable with it. Because of this he gets away with murder where my parents are concerned. He stays out late, drinks a lot and get into all sorts of scrapes. When mum and dad tell him off he just laughs and carries on. The thing is he is pretty cool and though he's a bit of a troublemaker he's quite popular. I want to be like him – is that odd?

Alex says

Older brothers and sisters act as important role models to us. We often look up to them for guidance on how to behave at school, work, with family and with friends. However, they also have the ability to be negative influences, too. It's understandable that you want to be like your brother; he is rebellious, sociable and charming – traits that seem attractive and which you would like to possess. Unfortunately, his recent behaviour is nothing to copy. He may seem to be able to run rings round your mum and dad but he's going to have a shock when he discovers this kind of attitude won't be tolerated by other adults. If you want to be like him, try to be charming and clever, but add in some sense of respect and responsibility!

22 I just can't focus on my exam revision. Please help!

> My GCSEs are looming and I'm finding it really difficult to revise. I spend hours sat in my room staring at the book in front of me but nothing goes in! I get distracted easily by friends messaging me, music, TV or my little brother. I'm really worried I'm going to fail my exams and my mum will go mad.

Mohammed, 15

Alex says

Ask your mum for help organising your revision. The key to effective revision is to work in a room with enough space for your books, with no phone, TV, music (or little brothers) to distract you and with a timetable of topics to work to. It's no good just sitting down and flipping through a textbook – nothing will go in that way. Make a revision chart and plan what you intend to revise. Budget enough of the remaining study time you have left to cover all the important areas. Make some flashcards and write the information down rather than just reading it. This is a far more effective way of getting the information to stick. Then use the flashcards to test yourself. Use revision tricks like making up mnemonics to help you remember lists or dates. It is hard work but it will be worth the effort when you get your results in the summer!

23 Should I leave school at 16?

I'm 16 next year and my mum wants me to go sixth-form college because that's what my brothers and sister did. I'm not so sure. I get decent marks at school but I don't enjoy it as much as some of my friends. Also I like the idea of making my own money. I'm interested in doing an apprenticeship because I've heard that you can learn and get paid at the same time. Mum says I can always do that once I've got some A levels and that I will be at a disadvantage if I leave early. Is she right? How do I make this decision?

Nishin, 15

Alex says

Since the government has raised the school leaving age in stages you will be required to remain in full-time education or training until the age of 18. This is because research shows that young people who carry on learning or training until the age of 18 are likely to earn more money, remain generally healthier and get in less trouble with the police. However this doesn't mean your only option is to stay in school and do A-levels. You can do a working apprenticeship. This would give you on-the-job experience and you would receive a limited salary for the work you do. If you aren't sure exactly what work to pursue in life, you can do a diploma, which gives the broader skills needed for a variety of careers. Or, failing that, if you know exactly what you prefer, you can choose to do a vocational training course that gives the skills needed for a specific career. Ultimately, what you do with your future is your decision; there is no right or wrong answer as long as you make an informed choice from the available options.

I chose to leave school and do an apprenticeship and it was the best decision I ever made. I've been getting paid while learning a trade that's going to mean I can be independent f or the rest of my life.
Jed, 17

It's down to the individual. I personally enjoyed education and achieving A-levels was important to me. I'm going to university next year and can't wait to start my course. I can see that education isn't for everyone though.
Louis, 18

I couldn't really decide on what I wanted to do so did a diploma. It helped me develop my skill sets and I think I'm in a better position now to choose what I want to do.
Abdul, 18

I think A-levels are important. There's something to be said for academic education. I enjoyed doing them and feel I learned a lot. There's still time after to do an apprenticeship as well if you want.
James, 19

It Happened to Me

My mum and dad didn't go to university and so weren't thrilled when I announced that I was thinking of applying! My dad grumbled that I would just be wasting 3 years of my life when I should be working to build up important job experience. I listened to what they had to say because they've both had great careers themselves, but I also researched the options that were available to me. Of course, university isn't all about getting a job. There is a value in just gaining more education even if it's not directly applicable to the workplace, but of course it really helps if the thing you specialise in makes you more employable. I was always good at chemistry and after some research online found that a chemistry degree can lead to some really good career options. To get into university I needed A-levels so that was my next step. I ended up getting good grades because I had focused on what I wanted to achieve. The good news is this has meant I have had three offers from the universities I applied to.

Dominic, 18

What's In A Relationship?

Alex says

Close encounters of the relationship kind...

Relationships are not always for everyone. Or not necessarily in our teen years anyway. We're all different and we want different things from life, but if and when you do develop feelings for someone it's good to have some confidence and self awareness.

So picture this; you're sitting in the school canteen and all of a sudden the most amazing person you've ever seen appears before you. You'd love to strike up conversation immediately but all you manage to do is muster up a shy smile, then spend the rest of the day wishing you were brave enough to even to speak to them.

It's difficult to walk up to a complete stranger and talk to them out of the blue. If you're going to do it, then it needs to feel natural and not forced. Making eye contact is one of the best ways to register on their radar. It's also a great way to judge how they feel about you. Take a deep breath, make eye contact with them and smile.

Try to find out something about this person: what music, sports and hobbies they like, where they live, what makes them tick. In this way, the next time you see them there will be something you can mention to break the ice and start up a conversation. For example, what have the two of you got in common? If you are both at the same school, then this is a good starting point. You can ask about favourite subjects or teachers, or what's edible in the canteen. As soon as you get chatting the situation will gain momentum. Body language and responses to what you say will let you know if the conversation is worth continuing. If they start looking over your shoulder while you are chatting it may be a sign that they don't want to continue (or it may just be that they are late for their next French lesson!)

Remember to listen to what they say and not talk at the same time. Don't try and impress with bold or braggish statements – there's nothing more unattractive than arrogance and first impressions count for a lot. Just relax, keep calm and be as confident as you possibly can, even if you don't feel it on the inside.

24 I need to look good or my girlfriend might leave me!

I finally got up the courage to ask a girl out that I've liked for two whole years. I've never had a girlfriend before so I was amazed when she agreed to go out with me. Now all I can think about is how she might leave me if I don't look right. Until recently my mum bought all my clothes for me from a catalogue and I've never thought much about hairstyles or my 'image'. I know it's not all about looks and what you wear, but some of the other guys at school really seem to spend time on how they look. Is it important? I really don't want her to go off me!

George, 15

Alex says

You've done the really difficult part. You found the courage to approach this girl and ask her out. And, hey – guess what? She said yes! There's nothing to be afraid of now except yourself. The fact is that she likes you. So stop any negative feelings in their tracks and get on with just enjoying getting to know this girl.

You're obviously feeling anxious about your appearance, hair and clothes but honestly these are secondary items. She's going out with YOU – not with your jeans or your haircut. Obviously you need to be washed and groomed; it's good to be clean and smell fresh, but what made her agree to seeing you in the first place was that she likes you! All you need do now is show her that you are thoughtful, reliable, considerate and fun to be with. So don't get hung up on what your clothes are like or what your hair is doing; just relax and enjoy each other's company.

It's a great feeling to find out the girl of your dreams feels the same way. But don't overthink things and don't get too intense or worried. Just relax, treat her as best as you can and things are sure to go well!
Grayson, 14

Start choosing your own clothes now! You need to build up your confidence and sense of who you are – and you should start with this.
Gabe, 15

Looking good for your girlfriend certainly matters a bit but what's much more important is that you treat her well. If she leaves you despite this, then at least you can be sure you did the best you could and it wasn't meant to be.
Jonny, 15

25 I've fallen in love on Facebook. What should I do?

Justin, 15

> I know it sounds weird but I have found my ideal woman on Facebook. I don't know her that well but she is everything I'd like in a girlfriend. The trouble is she's 20 and I am only 15. I wish there was some way we could be together. I keep dreaming about her and wishing we could meet up sometime. I've seriously never seen anyone who is so perfect in my whole life before!

Alex says

A word of caution: what you see online is not always a reality. Keep in mind that ANYBODY could be behind a Facebook profile so be extremely careful when chatting with people online. Also, NEVER agree to meet up with someone you have met only through Facebook! Though this is happening online, what you're experiencing is an old-fashioned crush. What's the difference? Well, love is two-way. When it's love the other person usually responds to your feelings. Crushes are different. You might have a crush on a teacher, a TV presenter or even your mum's best friend. Crushes are perfectly natural (kind of like a dress rehearsal for the real thing later on), but you have to prepare yourself for the fact that the feelings are just in your head. Frankly, you don't know this person and even if she is who she <u>says</u> she is, she's too old for you. Forget about this crush and focus instead on the real world for a while. Soon you will meet someone who is more your age and who wants to be with you.

26 I think I'm in love. How can I tell if it's real?

> How do you know when you're in love? I've been seeing my girlfriend for two weeks now and I think about her every minute of the day. I want to tell her how I feel but I'm worried it's too soon. I talked to my older brother about it and he said it wasn't love but it was just a crush. Is he right?

Tom, 13

Alex says

Whether it's really is true love or a crush you obviously have very strong feelings for your girlfriend. However, you are still very young and falling in love takes time and is usually based on two people getting to know each other through ups and downs over quite a long period. I suggest that don't rush into telling your girlfriend you love her until you are 100% sure it's what you're feeling. For now, plan some fun outings, on your own or in a group, such as a trip to the cinema or bowling alley. Get to know each other and just see what happens, and remember not to put pressure on yourself. Relationships in your early teens are really just close friendships, so relax and enjoy yourselves!

✷ DO Wait before deciding how you feel. It's early days.

✷ DON'T Rush into saying 'I love you' until you're sure you mean it.

27 My best friend competes with me for girls' attention

My problem is that my best friend always moves in on every girl I like. I used to think it wasn't on purpose because the first few times we both met the girl at the same time. Since then it seems each time I have a crush on a girl she becomes his next target. It's really starting to get to me. The thing is I'm not bad looking but he's better looking and good at chatting to girls. I'm sick of always coming second. What can I do to change things?

Dinesh, 14

Alex says

If your friend was deliberately trying to spoil your relationships, I'd say get a new friend. I suspect, however, that what you describe is simply blokey competition. That doesn't mean you should put up with it. Why not talk to him and tell him it's annoying you? Point out that you wouldn't behave like this towards him, so what gives him the right to walk all over your feelings? And, remember, with the right girl then it doesn't matter if he's better at attracting girls than you – because the right girl is naturally going to prefer you. On the other hand, if you're just worried about him cramping your style, when you are hoping to meet new girls then maybe you should consider leaving him behind next time. Chatting to girls can be hard enough without your best mate trying to put you off.

28 I'm scared if I dump her I'll lose all my friends

I've been seeing a girl for the last six months during which time I've grown really close with all of her friends. We all get on great and I really don't want to lose them as mates if things don't work out with my girlfriend. These days we fight a lot and I don't feel as happy as I used to. Do you think there's any chance her mates will want to stay friends with me if I break up with her?

Josh, 16

Alex says

The friends you describe came with the relationship and were hers to begin with, so it's unrealistic to expect that you can end things with her and keep all her best mates. This doesn't mean you should stay with her when you don't want to. Life is about change and sometimes you have to endure upheaval. If you are genuinely close with these people then hopefully they will understand your motives and the need to move on. They might not be available to spend so much time with — because they may have to prioritise their friendship with your girlfriend first, but they aren't going to hate you. The best thing you can do is to end things as nicely as possible and then give her the space she needs. When the dust has settled there's no harm in seeing if there's room for you all to be friends again. Good luck!

29 My girlfriend's dumped me and my world has fallen apart!

My girlfriend finished with me last week and I've been in a state. I can't stop feeling a pressure, like a big lump in my chest and just as it's going away I think of her and it comes straight back. I was so happy with the way things were going. Why did she have to end things with me? I didn't cheat on her, I paid her compliments and I tried to be kind and supportive all the time. She's going out with a really popular sporty guy now (who is really different from me) and I just don't understand what she sees in him! Why did she have to end it?

Alix, 15

Alex says

Why did she end it? Pick from the following selection of reasons. Because she could/she got bored/she's young/she's a bit shallow/she didn't feel the same way you did/she wants to be with a sporty guy – or perhaps nobody on the planet will ever know, including her! The best advice I can give you is to make a clean break of it and engineer it so that you don't see her for a while. Every time you see her or think about her, you reopen those old wounds. To get over someone you need to rediscover who you are inside – solo and independent. It sounds like a cliché now, but time will help you to see things differently. Hopefully you'll soon find that the pain gets less and things become more bearable. I believe there's someone out there for everyone but we often have to try out different relationships to find the right one. Keep being a kind and supportive person because sooner than you realise someone will come along who appreciates you and then your ex will just become a part of your history.

> I know it's not what you want to hear but she was clearly not the one for you. In a year's time you'll be with someone new and you'll realise that you would never have met them if you'd been with your ex.
> Leon, 15

> Break-ups are a horrible experience and I feel for you. She sounds like she's chucking a good guy – you deserve someone who appreciates you a bit more.
> Jarmain, 15

> Some girls never know when they've got a good thing going. Seek the support of your mates and go out and have a good time. You're only 15 so you have loads of time to find Mrs Right!
> Lin, 14

30 Can I trust my girlfriend after she cheated on me?

I found out that my girlfriend had cheated on me with another boy. When I confronted her she got angry and finished it between us. Now it's a month later and she keeps calling and begging me to take her back. I don't know if I can ever trust her again. It's really hard to say no because I still really like her and she keeps crying and telling me how sorry she is. Should I give her another chance?

Patrick, 15

Alex says

This is a tricky one. If you think she's genuinely sorry and you want to take the risk because you still like her, then perhaps give her another chance, but make it clear you won't put up with any further deceit. If you do decide to give her a chance, you'll also have to deal with the fact that it's going to take time to trust her again. Will you be able to relax without constantly worrying if she's with someone else behind your back? Can you forgive her enough to not question her all the time? These are the things to think about carefully before you take her back. Only you can make the decision.

DO Make it clear this is the last chance.

DON'T Let her walk all over you. You don't deserve to be cheated on.

31

Do you think she'd give me a second chance?

I dated a girl I really liked for 6 months. We got on really well but I ended up finishing with her because I met someone else. Things didn't work out with the new girl and now I'm on my own again. Do you think I should text my ex-girlfriend and ask if she would like to give things another go? Or would I just look really desperate?

Abioyne, 15

Alex says

You don't sound desperate but be honest with yourself before you approach her. Do you want to go back with her because you genuinely miss her company or because you have now found yourself on your own? If it's the latter, then move on and find someone new. Perhaps your ex-girlfriend has forgiven you for dropping her the first time around, but don't be surprised if she is quite cool towards you. She's been hurt once and is not going to be thrilled about the possibility of this happening again. It's probably best not to text her to ask her out again. Why don't you suggest meeting up and explain your feelings and do it face to face. After all, she will need some reassurance that you mean it this time.

32 Can you ever be good friends with your ex?

I'm 16 and have been in a relationship for the last two years but it ended badly. My girlfriend believed I had cheated on her when I'd only flirted with a girl in her class. We had a row and eventually I finished things between us. Now she thinks I'm the lowest form of life. We never speak face to face but I keep hearing that she says terrible things about me behind my back. Sometimes I wish I'd never met her. And then other times I start to miss her all over again. Is it possible to be friends with your ex?

Todd, 16

Alex says

Breaking up is difficult. People who go out together for months or years can develop strong feelings, which then get hurt when the relationship ends. It's oddly easy for love to turn sour and slip into hate; both are very powerful emotions. But it's also necessary for the love to disappear when two people do break up – at least for a time – or else how could they separate? For whatever reason, things went wrong between you two. She obviously felt enormously jealous, and has tried to make you feel that pain. It's probably unfair but that's how people are built. It's always harder for the person who gets dumped than the one doing the dumping but nobody escapes without some difficult and mixed feelings. To answer your question – yes, you can be friends with your ex, but not straight away. Give it some time. It's probably not likely to happen before she has rebuilt her confidence and self-esteem over a matter of weeks or months.

33 My best mate has a girlfriend and doesn't want to see me!

My best friend recently got a new girlfriend and wants to spend all his time with her. Our friendship of 3 years obviously counts for nothing because every time I invite him out somewhere he's too busy seeing her. I also don't really get on too well with her and think she feels the same way about me!

Joey, 14

Alex says

I can see how hard it must seem to you. He's having this fantastic new experience and you're not. What's even worse is that he doesn't seem to want you along for the journey. Quite naturally you feel totally abandoned and you miss your friend. New relationships can take up a lot of time but he may need you to gently remind him that friendships require maintenance, too. Maybe sitting down and talking to him about it will make him realise how neglected you feel. Explain that you're happy that he's found someone he really likes, but that you miss his company and would like to see him a bit more. But do be prepared for him to be too high on the 'love drug' to change for a little while. He wouldn't be the first person that has ever sacrificed one close friend for another, but true friends stick around, so just bide your time.

Are you ready for a relationship?

Some people spend the whole of their teens going from relationship to relationship, while others find themselves single until their twenties. When it comes to relationships, there are no hard and fast rules. Some people get lucky the first time and others spend ages finding the right person. If you are desperate for a relationship, then you need to ask yourself why. Are you hoping they will solve all the problems in your life? Do you think having a relationship will make you less lonely? Give you someone to show off? Make you seem more attractive? Or more popular with your friends? If any of these are your reasons for wanting to be in a relationship then you need to think again.

So you've met a wonderful person and the two of you have hit it off. Things are happening between you; you've been out together and enjoyed each other's company. But what next? The first thing to consider is whether your needs are the same. Are you ready for something serious or do you both want to keep things light-hearted? If both of you are over 16 (the legal age of consent in the UK), are you looking for a sexual relationship?

People rarely settle down in their teens. There's an awful lot of other life going on at the same time. Your friendships are very important to you, and then there's family, school, exams and hobbies to think about, too. So try to find out how much you really have in common, and whether you are on the same page about the friendship. The key to dealing with dating is to introduce your new partner to your friends and family as soon as possible. That way they won't be seen as a threat to your time, friendship, hobbies, schoolwork etc!

Relationships can be tricky things to negotiate; they take an awful lot of effort and honesty. But when you are together, try to relax. This means, don't worry about doing stuff wrong or about what the other person thinks of you all the time. Everyone says or does the wrong thing sometimes, and everyone makes embarrassing mistakes from time to time. Whatever you do, don't worry about the future, because that means that you are not concentrating on enjoying the present. Enjoy your time with your new friend, and don't get all over-anxious about whether or not there will be more dates!

One day you will pair off with someone seriously. Then you may have to make decisions between love and your other friendships. But that may not happen until your twenties or even later, so the best way to use this time is to get to know yourself and the person you are.

We can't help who we fall in love with and if you find yourself attracted to someone of the same sex, don't just lock up your feelings and try to be someone you aren't. If you don't feel you can tell someone you know, then speak to one of the organisations in the Get Connected! section on pages 94-95. They can help you work through your mixed feelings about yourself.

34 I'm in love with someone but she already has a boyfriend!

I met an amazing girl while I was at a basketball match last week. When we chatted it felt like there was a connection between us. We couldn't stop talking the whole evening. It was only after that I found out she has a boyfriend. I was gutted and I don't know what to do. I've never met anyone like her but I'm not the sort to try to break up other people's relationships. Please help!

Andrei, 14

Alex says

We all have moments where we can find someone else attractive, and she's probably no exception. But if you respect her at all you won't push the boundaries right away. Give her time to notice you and perhaps get to like you. I would suggest you stay friends with her and keep it light-hearted and fun. Then it will seem natural one day for you to say something like: 'I know you're spoken for, but I wish you weren't...' If she likes you enough, she can choose to end her current relationship on her own terms.

DO Respect her boundaries – stay in the friend zone.

DON'T Put her in a difficult position. If she likes you it's up to her to decide.

Being Independent But Staying Safe!

Alex says

Out and about & keeping yourself safe

One of the best things about being a teenager is that you gain some independence and can start to venture out without your folks in tow! Your new-found independence can be a whole lot of fun but there are lots of things you need to be aware of to make sure you stay safe. Here are some practical tips for while you are out and about on your own or with friends:

Before you go out, make sure you plan where you are going and how you are going to get back. Let someone in charge know your destination and when you plan to be home. Parents, carers and other family members can usually be called upon to collect you, especially when you first start going out – and this is no bad thing, because getting home late at night can sometimes be a challenge.

Don't make eye contact with people who are behaving strangely or aggressively, or are drunk. Make sure you stay with your group and don't leave anyone behind. If anyone in your group gets insulted, picked on for a fight or called names, it's best to ignore it rather than retaliate. It's better to be safe than foolishly brave.

Never accept a lift home from a stranger or from someone you suspect has been drinking. If you're unable to get home, rather than do something drastic, call a family member or someone you can trust to help you out.

Stay alert to your surroundings whether you are walking on the street, on a bus or with your friends. Try to avoid walking alone at night, but if do, walk with a confident stride and look as if you know where you are going.

Keep your phone out of sight as much as you can and if someone asks to see your phone or borrow it to make a call, think twice about whether they are likely to snatch it off you. Mobile phone muggings are an increasingly common crime especially among teenage boys. The majority of muggings occur between 6pm and midnight, so avoid being alone on the street or travelling on public transport late at night.

This is a no-brainer, but stick to well-lit roads and avoid shortcuts through wooded areas, car parks or alleyways.

Don't leave any bags or other possessions unattended and this include drinks, in case anyone has the idea to 'spike' it with alcohol or another drug.

Above all, trust your own judgement! Don't let other people persuade you to do anything or go anywhere you don't want to. If you feel uneasy about a situation, then try to remove yourself from it as soon as you can. If your 'gut instinct' tells you a situation is wrong, go with it – because it's usually right!

35 My dad won't let me go to parties. I feel left out!

> I'm 15 but my dad won't let me go to house parties at the weekends. He says I'm too young and that we can talk about it again when I'm 16. I get really angry with him because I can't wait that long. I'm missing out on the best years of my life now!

Tadgh, 15

Alex says

I know it seems unfair to you but your dad is only trying to keep you safe. His intention is not to ruin your life. My suggestion is to comply with his wishes now on the understanding that, over a period of time, he should gradually trust you to stay out a bit later. This display of maturity is precisely the sort of thing that will raise his confidence because he'll know you're appreciating and understanding the risks. Every time you ridicule his concerns or be rude to your dad you are only confirming his belief that you are not mature enough to be trusted. Talk to him and say you'll go along with his views, but ask if he will review the situation in 6 months' time.

DO Abide by his wishes now, and show your maturity.

DON'T Confirm his beliefs that you are not old enough to be trusted!

36 My dad says my best friend is a bad influence!

> My best friend has his ears pierced and hair shaved, so my dad thinks he's a bad influence on me! The truth is James is really popular and it has really helped my confidence. My dad is very conservative and believes that anyone who looks slightly out of the ordinary is bad news. Nothing I say seems to make a difference. How can I stop him being so narrow-minded?

Alfie, 15

Alex says

It can be really tough when your family disapproves of someone whom you think is great. As you say, your dad may be quite conservative and perhaps your friend didn't make the best first impression on him. However even the most conservative minds can be changed given the right reasons. The key thing here is communication. Talking through your reasons for liking a person is really good way to make your family see things from your perspective. Ultimately, what they care about is you and your safety. If you can demonstrate that your friend watches out for you and your confidence has grown because of him, then hopefully your dad will eventually get behind your friendship.

 DO Calmly explain your point of view. Communication is the key.

DON'T Forget that they care about you and your safety.

37 I'm too shy to dance. What should I do?

> Whenever we go to a party or under-16s night I just freeze up and can't dance even though most of my friends dance and chat to girls all night long. I sit at the side feeling like the odd one out. I wish I knew how to dance but I don't and I'm too embarrassed to ask any of my mates to show me. Please help!

Zain, 15

Alex says

Dancing isn't necessarily about your technique – it's all about being confident. Most people you see dancing haven't learned a dance step and have little more experience than you. Start with a song that you like, then just relax and try to get into the rhythm of it. Practice on your own in your bedroom at home first, but any girls watching you are looking at body language and confidence over dancing ability. Even if you feel a bit silly at first it doesn't matter. Whatever happens, don't get bogged down with your insecurities, just grab the opportunity to experiment with dancing and have some fun!

DO Relax and enjoy yourself. No-one is looking at you.

DON'T Overthink your moves!

38 I'm not interested in going out. Am I odd?

> I'm not interested in having a social life. I like to spend my time reading and being online – usually playing games or programming. I get called a geek at school but it doesn't really bother me. There's so much pressure at school to go out and meet girls but I just don't see what's so great about it. It all sounds like a waste of time to me. Is it normal to feel like this?

Colm, 15

Alex says

Not all boys are social animals and there's nothing wrong with having an interest in computers – or any other hobby for that matter. Your friends at school are all very excited because they are having their first big social experiences, but people develop socially in different ways. Don't let their comments affect you. As you get older, you'll discover the ways that YOU enjoy being social and will have your own fantastic experiences. Computer programming and reading are brilliant pastimes to cultivate and can make you more employable in later life – so for now your time is certainly being put to good use.

✳ **DO** Be happy in your own skin – there's nothing wrong with who you are.

✳ **DON'T** Let other peoples' small-minded comments upset you.

39 How do I ditch a friend I don't like anymore?

Jin Lo, 16

> I made friends with this boy because I was new to the school and didn't know anyone. I was aware that he also didn't have many mates, but I didn't know why, but after getting to know him better it became apparent why! He borrows money from me all the time and doesn't pay it back, and from what others have told me, I don't think he's very loyal to me as a friend. I don't know how to tell him I don't want to be his friend any more. I know it sounds mean but he's not someone I would have made friends with if I'd known all this from the start.

Alex says

If you have good reasons for the way you feel then the best thing you can do is make your feelings clear to him. Obviously you need to try and avoid being nasty as you don't want to destroy his confidence, but it sounds like you have genuine grievances so I think you have every right to voice them. From what you describe he has brought his dodgy reputation on himself through his behaviour. You don't ever HAVE to be friends with anyone you don't want to be. Make it clear to him that you feel things have changed and you don't want to give him the wrong impression about your friendship — but that you are moving on. There are tricky conversations like this to be had throughout life but running away from them only makes them worse in the long run.

DO Make your feelings clear.

DON'T Avoid having the tricky conversation.

40 My group of friends make me seem invisible to girls!

All of my friends are quite sporty and fit looking. I'm quite short for my age and a little bit overweight. When we go out as a group, girls talk to them and I get ignored. No one seems to notice me or even realise I'm there. I'm starting to think the only way to get noticed is to hang out with a new group of friends who don't make me invisible to girls!

Chaz, 14

Alex says

At 14, your body is still developing, almost on a daily basis – as are those of your friends. You say you are quite short and a bit overweight now, but you are not likely to stay that way. Most people in their early 20s are unrecognisable from the way they looked when they were 14. You'll also find that peoples' attitudes change as they mature, and that the things many girls find attractive right now won't be the same in a few years' time. As far as finding new friends is concerned, I think your solution is a little extreme. It's not looks girls notice but confidence. Therefore, try to focus on your personal strengths. For example, you've made a circle of friends already. Work out what it is they like about you and use this to feel more positive. As you begin to realise there's nothing wrong with you, you'll walk taller and stop feeling invisible.

41

Is it true that girls like tough guys?

Will being tough make me more attractive to girls? My brother used to be really slim but then he started going to the gym and hanging out with a different bunch of guys. He says that they get into fights on Saturday nights sometimes. He thinks that girls prefer tough guys. Is he right?

Lawrie, 14

Alex says

It's a common misconception that being 'tough' will make you more attractive to girls. I can't tell you how many girls have written to me over the years complaining that boys waste their time, money and energy trying to be the tough guy because they think it'll make them seem more attractive and manly. In fact, for many girls, boys who are prone to violence and who are aggressive are a huge turn-off. The key point here is that aggression and violence don't make you attractive to anyone. There are lots of myths about what girls like, usually perpetrated by guys trying to prove a point about themselves. The fact is for every girl that likes a tough guy, there are hundreds more that like funny guys, short guys, tall guys, clever guys and sporty guys. In fact everyone likes someone different so just be yourself as that's really what girls want.

42 I get called 'gay' at school even though I'm not.

> My problem is I'm always being called gay at school even though I'm not. It started when I defended the idea of gay marriage in a class debate and now everyone thinks I'm gay. It doesn't help that I usually do well in exams, so I often get called 'swot', too. Can you help me? It's making me miserable and want to avoid going to school at all.

Joe, 15

Alex says

It is never a good feeling to get falsely accused about anything. And despite recent progress and a change in the law, there is still a widespread prejudice against homosexuality. Bear in mind that the those who criticise gay people are ignorant and could be afraid of being gay themselves. Another reason why your classmates have a go is that they're already a bit jealous of you for being more academically successful than them. The truth is you're obviously quite a success. The best way to stop people teasing you is to deny them the satisfaction of getting a reaction out of you. If you can ignore these remarks, simply smile at the people who make them and show that you are enjoying your own life anyway. They will eventually lose interest and these rumours will die of their own accord.

43 My best friend was mugged for his phone!

Last week my best friend was followed home from the bus station and when he turned into a side street a guy pulled out a knife and demanded his phone and cash. He did as he was told and then got pushed to the ground and threatened not to tell anyone. The man ran off; my friend went home in shock and I've hardly seen him since. This has also shaken me up and I'm now constantly watching my back when I go out. The rest of us are really paranoid that this might happen to us next.

Adam, 14

Alex says

Your friend had an awful experience but did the right thing by handing his phone over. He's lost a phone (which can be replaced), and he's lost some social confidence, but he avoided any further physical harm, which is the most important thing. The most likely person to be mugged in the street is a teenage boy – usually by another teenage boy. The best thing you can do for your friend right now is to offer words of support and be there for him when he feels ready to see people again. Show him the 'Out and about & keeping yourself safe' advice on page 66-67 and help him to build up his confidence again. In the meantime, some useful advice is to keep your phone out of sight as much as you possibly can, and try to avoid walking alone on the street, especially at night. Why don't you try to arrange to get home together in a group? You need to be sensible and vigilant, but if the worst happens, remember that a phone can always be replaced, but YOU can't!

> I don't blame your friend for feeling traumatised. If someone pulls a knife on you, then give them what they want. There's no point being a hero over a phone!
> Simon, 15

> It's unlikely he or you will get mugged again anytime soon but I think this letter raises an important issue. As a teenage boy, being robbed is more common than many people think. Be safe!
> Pablo, 14

> I try to avoid using my phone in public as much as possible these days. Someone could follow you off a train or bus, so be vigilant.
> Victor, 14

CHAPTER ONE

44

Can you help? I'm no good at chatting to girls!

> Every time I try to chat to a girl at school she just roll their eyes at me and tell me to go away. I'm not bad looking but I don't understand how chatting to girls is supposed to work. Is it the same as chatting to boys? Can you help?

Dion, 14

Alex says

If you approach it in a relaxed way, without putting too much pressure on yourself, then chatting to girls is the same as chatting to boys! We're all human beings with (mostly) the same motivations and feelings. But I do agree that it can be hard to chat to girls who are complete strangers. It's easier when you already know them from school or from a sports club, for example. However, the best way to make a good impression is to just be completely natural. Most people like to be asked questions about themselves, so start with some simple ways in to a conversation by asking her about school, hobbies, where she lives, her brothers and sisters, what she does at the weekends etc. The girl you mention in your letter may not be interested in striking up conversation with you, but many other girls will. So relax, take a deep breath and just go for it!

Chapter Five

Sex, Drugs & All That Stuff

Alex says

Planet S.E.X.

As a teenage boy it's likely that sex is on your mind a lot. Perhaps you're worried about your sexual feelings or that everyone is doing it but you, or maybe you're afraid that you're going to be a virgin forever. It's also likely that you've seen pornographic images. While this has probably shown you a fair bit about how your body responds to sexual stimulation, please do remember that it's not a realistic depiction of the female or male body, sex or relationships.

Pornography is a fantasy based on fake imagery, fake pleasure and fake scenarios. In the world of porn no one is ever shy about their bodies, all women have big breasts and all men have a large penis. No one is shy or afraid of getting it wrong or unconfident about what they are doing. In the real world sex is very different.

The problem with watching porn regularly as a boy is how it can make you think that girls and women are there for your indulgence, regardless of their feelings. They become bodies rather than people. If you want sex with a real person, first of all you have to get them to like you!

These are the facts. Sex with a consensual partner above the age of 16 is about mutual affection and exploration. It is a way to bring two people closer. It bonds couples together and is an important ingredient in any long lasting relationship. It's not a sport; nor a showing-off contest. Good sex is about pleasing the other person, being sensitive to their needs and showing them love and respect. It is a natural part of life and is how nearly all of us got here in the first place. It's how we make babies but it's also something couples do for pleasure.

And then there's the downside. Un-safe sex – which is sex without a form of contraception such as a condom – can lead to unwanted pregnancy and sexually transmitted infections (STIs). Some of these are worse than others. Chlamydia and gonorrhoea for instance can lead to infertility if they go untreated but are relatively easy for doctors to treat. HIV/AIDS is a sexually transmitted infection that is passed on through blood, semen or vaginal fluids and is less easy to treat. The problem is that many STIs have no symptoms so you need to get checked out (see the Get Connected! section on page 94 for advice sources on sexual health) if you have had sex without a condom. This way you'll be sure that you won't pass it on the next time you have sex.

The most sensible precaution is obviously to practise safe sex by wearing a condom. This is a thin latex sheath that rolls over the penis and creates a barrier that prevents the man passing on his sperm to the woman and protects you from most sexually transmitted infections. Condoms are considered to be roughly 90% effective in shielding you from infections – so you'd be crazy not to use them.

45 All my friends brag about having sex

I'm sixteen and nearly all my mates go into detail about what has happened the night before with a girl. I feel like I'm the odd one out and it makes me look dumb. Is there something wrong with me or is it them just bragging about their experiences?

Anthony, 16

Alex says

Once you are over the age of 16 (which is the age of consent in the UK) losing your virginity shouldn't be a race, and being the first to do it certainly doesn't win you a prize. It's possible that some of your friends may be telling the truth, but many others are just as likely to be making it up so they don't look like the odd one out. There's nothing wrong with taking your time to have your first sexual experience. It's your body and it's your life. Wait until YOU feel ready and make sure don't end up ruining the experience in your hurry to get it out of the way. Research suggests that the average age of first sexual intercourse in the UK is 17 for boys. These statistics show despite what other lads might say, there is no need to rush into sex. But if and when you do have sex, make sure you use contraception to prevent STIs as well as unwanted pregnancy.

46 Should I post rude pictures of my ex-girlfriend?

Ravi, 16

Two weeks ago, my girlfriend and I broke up because she cheated on me with one of my friends after telling me she was ill. Since then she has tried to get back with me but when I said it was too late, and I couldn't forgive her for cheating on me, she texted a topless picture of herself fooling about with my friend. I hate what she's done to me, but another friend has suggested that I post it online to get my revenge. This would hurt her as much as she's hurt me, but deep down I know it's wrong.

Alex says

I understand you feel sad and sore but taking revenge in this way is not going to solve anything, and yes, it's wrong. Hurting her won't kill your pain – it just adds to the sum total of human misery. Both you and your ex also need to think hard about the dangers of 'sexting' (which is what this is). For example, if your ex happened to be under 16 and you forward a sexual picture of her to an internet address, you could be breaking the child pornography laws. You could find yourself prosecuted and on the Sex Offender's Register. You both also need to remember that the internet is forever! Some pictures sent in private but posted in public have caused girls to become horribly bullied and in extreme cases driven to harm themselves. I would put aside my vengeful feelings and explain to your ex how hurtful her behaviour has been. Delete the image from your phone, then tell her what you have done and how she needs to think hard about whether to do this kind of thing again. A lesser person than you may have gone ahead and posted the picture, so congratulate yourself on being the bigger person in this situation!

47 I'm worried that I might be addicted to pornography

Whenever I'm online I can't help clicking onto porn websites. Sometimes I spend hours doing it! I'm worried my family will find out. The other day I forgot to delete my search history and panicked because my sister also uses the same computer. I'm confused because the films I watch are very exciting and yet I don't feel in control of myself. Some of the stuff is pretty nasty, too and makes me feel awful for days. Is there something really wrong with me?

Ben, 16

Alex says

Unfortunately, as you've discovered, most pornography distorts and dehumanises our sexuality and relationships, but fortunately it isn't addictive in the way that drugs are. Yes, you get an adrenaline rush, but you wouldn't suffer withdrawal symptoms if you stopped doing it. You would need to find something else to do with your spare time, but nothing more serious than this. Pornography is harmful because it teaches you to ignore human feelings. In the real world, people have wishes and preferences about those they fall for. If you believe girls will just have sex with you because you want them to, then you are going to be greatly disappointed. Finally, sex with a real person is far better. So my advice to you is to not overthink your issues with pornography, but try to cut down looking at it and hopefully drop the habit. In the meantime, put more energy into finding a real partner with whom you can experience a loving and respectful relationship.

48 I keep getting erections in the most embarrassing situations!

> I keep getting erections and I don't know why. It's embarrassing and happens in weird places. It happened yesterday on the bus, but also when I wake up, sometimes in class and when I'm watching TV. There's nothing I can do about it. Sometimes my friends spot it and have a laugh at me, which makes me feel like I'm weird.

Damil, 14

Alex says

First of all, don't feel uncomfortable about what's happening; it's totally normal and you are not alone. Erections are a normal part of growing up. During puberty, many boys experience untimely erections sometimes fuelled by sexual thoughts, sometimes not. It is perfectly normal for boys your age to wake up with an erection. It happens because during the active part of sleep known as REM, hormones are released and, your penis is stimulated by these hormones. As for controlling them the best way is to try and relax and think about something totally non-sexual, like homework, a teacher you don't like or something that turns you off. Erections will go away with enough thought and as you get older, you'll find you will be able to control them much better.

49 Is it true that there are times when a girl can't get pregnant?

> Friends at school have told me there are safe times when you can have sex with a girl and she won't get pregnant. Is this true and if so is it really safe? I haven't had sex yet but I want to know because I don't like the idea of condoms. I've heard that you can't feel anything!

Chidi, 16

Alex says

There is no safe time to have unprotected sex. Have sex without a condom and you're always risking pregnancy and the possibility of contracting a sexually transmitted infection. It's possible that you may have heard of the so-called 'safe period' in a woman's cycle where she is less likely to get pregnant. This is not reliable for anyone, but especially so for teenagers as many younger women have irregular cycles. Don't risk it – ever! If you are planning on having sex always use a condom. Condom technology is advancing all the time and are designed so that you still feel sensation during sex. Try one by yourself and see! It doesn't feel 'numb' at all – far from it.

✳ **DO** Always use a condom!

✳ **DON'T** Listen to this idea – it's a myth!

50 How can I tell if I'm gay?

> I've always known I'm a bit different. I've never been very interested in girls and more recently have started having thoughts at night about other boys at school, and especially one of my friends who I feel really close to. Does this mean I'm gay and is there any way I can know for sure?

Luke, 16

Alex says

All you can know at this point is that you are curious about your sexuality and that you are not 100% sure if you are gay, straight or bisexual. Your teenage years can be about experimenting and trying out lots of different versions of your identity, from music and fashion to sexuality. It's only by doing this that we can find out who we are and rule out who we are not. It may well be that you discover you are gay and are attracted to men. Or you might discover through experimentation that you were simply curious and you become more interested in girls. Either way all that's important is that you get the peace of mind of discovering the real you now. If you feel you need further support in any way, do contact the helpline listed in the Get Connected! section on pages 94–95.

51

I'm worried about my binge drinking!

I am worried that I may have a problem. For the last 6 months or so I've been drinking cider with a bunch of friends almost every weekend. I've been sick while we're drinking and also sick the next day. I have headaches a lot these days and my schoolwork is starting to suffer. But I'm worried I might already have become an alcoholic. Is there a way to tell? How can I stop?

Usman, 16

Alex says

An alcoholic is someone who is drink-dependent with a physical desire for alcohol beyond all the rules of common sense. It's not a strictly scientific term, but more of an official view.

> I used to drink every day after school and ended up getting in a lot of trouble because I would do stupid things when I was drunk.
> Kavi, 16

Is there a pattern to your drinking that is getting out of control? Do you have a physical craving? It appears that you do have a pattern of binge-drinking which hasn't made you dependent on alcohol YET, but it could develop this way.

> You're not doing your body any favours. My brother was a drinker and was hospitalised. It's a horrible thing to do to yourself and you'll regret it if you take things too far.
> Faisal, 15

You appear to drink just to get drunk. This is a common pattern of behaviour among young adults but medical research has shown that it damages the brain, memory and your ability to control impulses towards violence. As you've found, it also makes you sick. I would strongly suggest knocking it on the head this weekend and see how much better you feel. If you find you genuinely can't stop yourself binge-drinking, then the next step is to visit your GP for help and advice. I have also given details of an advice group in the Get Connected! section on pages 94-95. Please contact them – they can help you get this sorted. Good luck.

> Alcohol damages your brain – it might seem like a harmless laugh but you're destroying the most important part of you!
> Anton, 15

52 My friend is trying to pressure me into smoking

> My best friend is always trying to get me to smoke. He pressures me when we are in front of our friends. It's really hard to say no. The other day we were all out together and he pulled out a cigarette and asked if I'd like to join him. When I said no he made it into a really big deal and kept asking why. I just wish he'd leave me alone as I really don't want to smoke.

Daniel, 14

Alex says

The next time he demands to know why simply say to him: 'Because I don't want to damage my body, which is my decision to make not yours'. Yes, he is putting you in a very difficult social position because there are lots of people who still think smoking is 'cool' (for some reason), and you want to save face in front of your mates. But silly peer pressure like this has started many young people on the road to dependency with regard to alcohol and tobacco. Standing up for yourself is the only way to fight back. No one with any common sense is going to think badly of you for saying no. If he carries on trying to belittle you or deride you in front of the group then point out the health warning on the cigarette packet. Hopefully a reminder of the disturbing image on most packs shows the kind of damage that smoking is doing to his body.

Alex says

As a teenage boy it can sometimes feel like there are a lot of challenges to face. Some can be great fun; others can seem like an ordeal while you are going through them. All of the issues you experience will help shape you into the adult you will one day become, and there is no experience that you can't learn something from. If there is one thing I would like you to take from reading this book it's that you will get the best out of your teen years by adopting a positive attitude and making sound and informed decisions. Think things through, don't give in to peer pressure and don't let the opinions of others affect the person you are inside.

Not all boys have to grow up to be the same kind of man. The world is full of different types of people! Remember this if someone tries to put you down or makes you feel bad about yourself. Being a teenage boy was the best experience I ever had and I really hope some of the things I learned can help benefit you, and make it the best time of your life, too. I sincerely hope you enjoy every moment of your teenage years!

Glossary

ABORTION is a medical procedure that is used to end (or terminate) a pregnancy.

ACNE is condition caused by overactive sebaceous glands in your skin which make your pores clog up and become infected.

ADRENALINE is a hormone that is responsible for the 'fight or flight' response to danger. Adrenaline is what kickstarts your system into action when you are under a threat, or believe that you are.

ANOREXIA is a mental condition that distorts your body image so that you see yourself as fat even if you are a normal weight or underweight.

ANTI-DEPRESSANTS can be prescribed by your doctor to help you when you're diagnosed with a very low mood or a depressive illness.

APPRENTICESHIP is a period of work training where you learn from an expert how to practice your craft or trade.

BISEXUAL(ITY) usually means feeling attracted to people of either sex.

COGNITIVE BEHAVIOURAL THERAPY (CBT) is a talking treatment for psychological problems like anxiety and mild depression.

CYBERBULLYING means bullying someone by text, on social media sites, via Twitter or any other app.

DEPRESSION is a state of low mood that can affect a person's thoughts and behaviour. Depressed people may feel sad, anxious, negative and empty and may be unable to focus on or concentrate on daily tasks and activities. Depression can be mild through to severe. Medication can be prescribed for depression, this is called anti-depressant medication.

ENDORPHINS are natural feel-good chemicals that are produced by the brain. Endorphins are often produced after periods of activity and exercise.

ERECTION refers to the aroused condition of a penis when it becomes engorged with blood and gets hard.

GAY usually means loving someone of your own sex.

HIV/AIDS are two different things. HIV is a virus that causes your body to attack itself and may prove fatal.

AIDS is the range of illnesses you may develop if you get HIV. Two ways of catching HIV are sexual contact, and sharing dirty needles to inject drugs.

HORMONES are chemical substances that the body naturally produces. Hormones trigger puberty, which is the developmental stage between childhood and adulthood.

INFATUATION an intense passion or love for someone, that may fairly shortlived.

INFERTILE means not being able to have children.

LIFE CYCLE refers to a series of stages of development most people experience in life, for example: childhood, teenage, adulthood

METABOLISM the chemical processes that take place in all living things in order to maintain life.

MNEMONICS are techniques that you can use to improve and help your memory. They are particularly useful for exams!

NUTRIENTS are substances in food and drink that are essential for life and growth of all living things.

PEER PRESSURE is the expectation that you will copy or be influenced by the attitudes and behaviour of your friends.

PROZAC is a prescription anti-depressant designed to raise your levels of the 'happiness' hormone in your body called serotonin.

PUBERTY is the name of the transition period when girls and boys begin to develop sexually.

SEXUALLY TRANSMITTED INFECTIONS (STIs) are infections you can catch from contact during sexual activity.

SEBUM is an oily substance secreted by glands in the skin to keep out water and germs. Sebum is produced by the sebaceous glands in the skin which are more active than usual during the teenage years.

STRENGTH TRAINING is a type of physical exercise which uses resistance to build strength, endurance and muscle.

VOCATIONAL COURSES prepare you to do a specific job in life, rather than giving you a general education.

VIRGINITY refers to when someone has never had sex.

Get Connected!

Violence or Abuse

Victim Support
www.victimsupport.org.uk
Helpline: 0845 30 30 900
This organisation gives free and confidential advice to victims of crime or anyone affected by crime.

ChildLine
www.childline.org.uk
Helpline: 0800 1111
Free national helpline for children and young people in danger or distress.

www.18u.org.uk
Free helpline: 0800 731 40 80
Support, information and helpline to young people under 18 who have experienced any type of abuse.

National Youth Advocacy Service
Email: help@nyas.net
www.nyas.net

Helpline: 0808 808 1001
Provides information, advice, advocacy and legal representation to young people up to the age of 25 through a network of advocates around England and Wales.

Rape Crisis for Boys and Young Men

Rape Crisis
www.rapecrisislondon.org/content/help-men-boys
Helpline: 0808 802 99 99
Originally established for women but also offers advice to boys and young men.

Contraception

Family Planning Association
www.fpa.org.uk/contraception-help/condoms-male-and-female
Offers specific advice on contraception, using condoms and where to get them.

Brook Advisory
www.brook.org.uk
Helpline: 0808 802 1234
The Brook specialises in helping young men and women with all sexual problems, including advice, contraception and abortion. On entering the home page, click on Ready for Sex and this leads into: contraception, having sex for the first time, unhealthy relationships and talking things through.

Bullying

Bullying
www.bullying.co.uk
Helpline: 0808 800 2222
This organisation deals with all types
of bullying in schools, including
cyberbullying.

Kidscape
www.kidscape.org.uk
Helpline for parents: 08451 205
204
Advises on bullying and child sex
abuse issues.

Alcohol

Alateen
www.al-anonuk.org.uk/alateen
To book a meeting: 020 7407 0215
Set up for teenage relatives and
friends of people with alcohol
problems.

Drugs

Frank
www.talktofrank.com
Helpline: 0300 123 6600
Friendly, confidential 24/7 drugs
advice service with access to live chat
and email via the website.

Gay

LLGS (London Lesbian and Gay Switchboard)
www.llgs.org.uk
Helpline: 0300 330 0630
Although 'London' is in the title the
helpline offers advice across the
country on gay, lesbian, bisexual and
transgender issues.

The Lesbian and Gay Foundation
www.lgf.org.uk
This website offers advice, support
and information.
Helpline 0845 3 30 30 30

Eating Disorders

Beat
www.b-eat.co.uk
Helpline: 0845 634 1414
Youthline: 0845 634 7650
Beat provides help and advice for
people with eating disorders including
anorexia, bulimia, binge eating and
compulsive overeating.

Index